AF411903

BOTTLE IN THE SMOKE

photographs by Jonathan Bayer

In the sleeping long ago
I hear the milkman's early horse
Stamp the packed and dirty snow.
I hear a neighbour's floating voice.

I hear the early milkman's horse
In summer cart the clinking crates,
And that forgotten, curling voice
Fades. Fades. Our day grows late.

Chinking in a cage of crates,
Small bottles by the classroom door
In the shouting playground wait,
Stuck with yellow slanting straws.

On rainy steps by midnight doors,
Those stalwart shapes are glimmering now,
And cross the disappearing years
From the sleeping long ago.

MARY SULLIVAN

Mine eyes fail for thy word, saying,

When wilt thou comfort me?

For I am become like

a bottle in the smoke. . .

(Psalm 119: 82–3)

MILK
INSIDE
IN
COOLER
PROPERTY OF
O & S C S

शीतल
आइस क्रीम

ASCOT
Creams Collection
MILK IN
Action
Ribena
Lucozade
ENERGY
SANDWICHES
LED ROLLS
DRINKS
RETTES

/22
ygold
METRIC
PACK
-15
IN

OWNERS RISK
PROP
DON'T FORGET
MINI TUES 31
603 5727
Kali SEPT 3. MERC
27th
R.15
SPARE PARTS
BROST FORGE LTD

Some circumstantial evidence
is very strong, as when you find
a trout in the milk.

(Henry David Thoreau)

WINSOR & NEWTON'S
NEW ART
POWDER COLOUR
RAW SIENNA

1a HOLLAND PARK AVE
TEL: 01-2...
1a2 LADBROKE GR...
...INVITE...
...MILY...

. . .he was half-way down
the area, edging his way through
a booby-trap of milk bottles.

(Margery Allingham,
More Work for the Undertaker)

He that shuns trifles must

shun the world.

(George Chapman)

NO PARKING

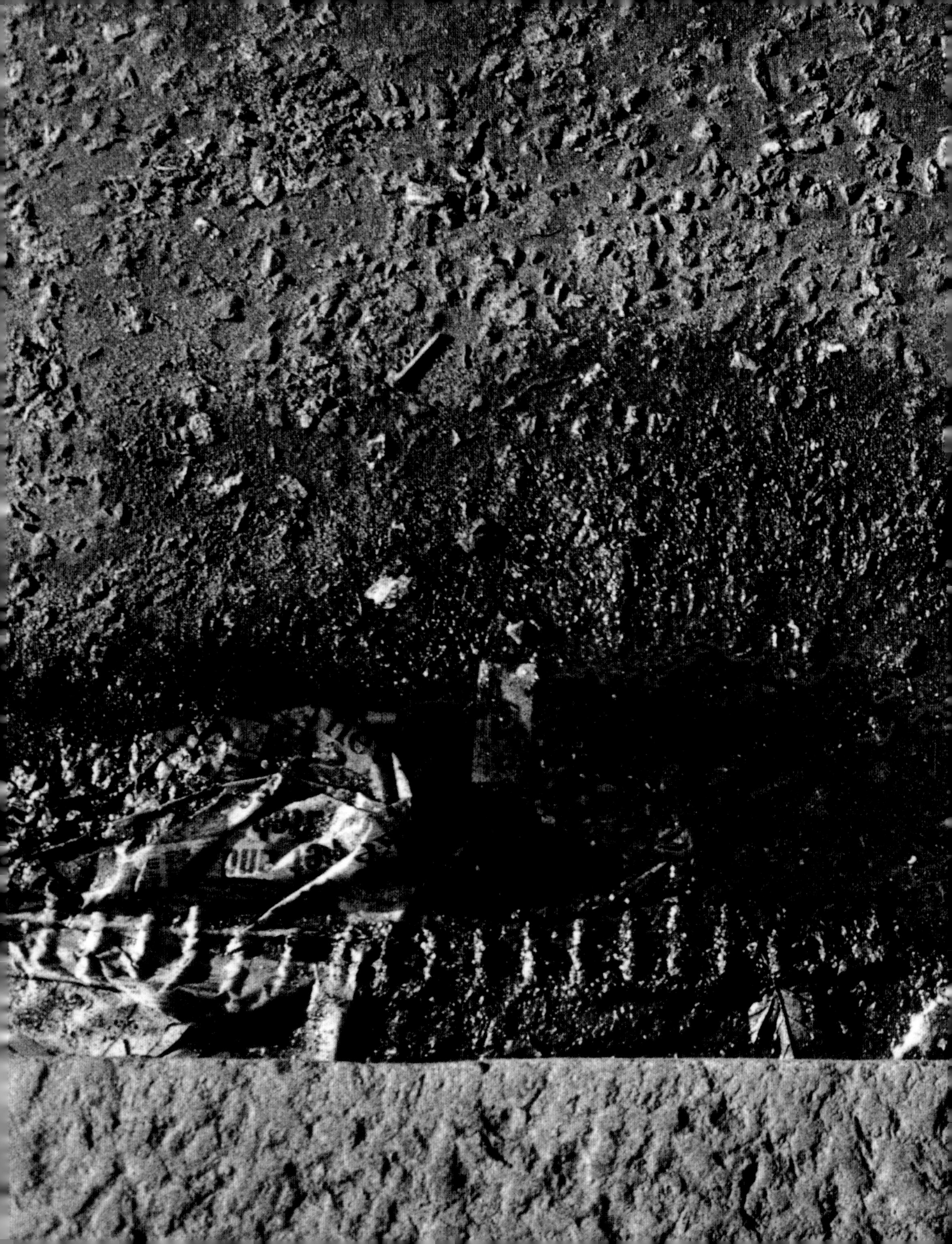

Evening
News

Weetabix
WHOLE WHEAT CEREAL
WITH EXTRA VITAMINS
THE WILTS FARM DAIRY
Owen & Son
THRIFTIES
LINCOLN BISCUITS
Rich Osbo
24
ANCHOR
MATURED
New Zealand
Cheddar Cheese
10 x 5.25oz P
daily pinta-
Kellogg's
Two Shakes
Kellogg's
CORN FLAKES
Yeoman
Varicety
ALL PURPOSE RICE
METRIC
375 gram
MILO
OVALTINE
AT JAIL
honey

Dairy Farmers
DAIRY
DAIRY
Weetabix
Weetabix
Weetabix
Weetabix
Weetabix
Weetabix
Weetabix
Walls
BACON
HEINZ
BAKED
BEANS
BIRDS
EYE
shop

SPURS
MANCHESTER
UNITED
FC
PICCADILLY
Britain's
finest
cigarette

Unigate
PLEASE RETURN

PLEASE DO NOT
LEAVE MILK BOTTLES
HERE Thank you.

Published in Great Britain by
JLB Publishing
7/29 Belsize Park
London NW3 4DX

ISBN 0 9540270 1 9

Photographs © Jonathan Bayer
Poem © Mary Sullivan

Design by LewisHallam
Printed and bound in Great Britain by
BAS Printers Limited, Salisbury